Skira**M**ini**ART**books

Fabio Isman

THE GHETTO

of Venice

SKIRA

Skira editore
SkiraMiniARTbooks

Editor
Eileen Romano

Design
Marcello Francone

Editorial Coordination
Carla Casu

Editing
Maria Conconi

Layout
Anna Cattaneo

Iconographical Research
Marta Tosi

Translation
Liam MacGabhann and Marco
Migotto for Language Consulting
Congressi, Milan

First published in Italy in 2010
by Skira Editore S.p.A.
Palazzo Casati Stampa
via Torino 61
20123 Milano
Italy

www.skira.net

Printed and bound in Italy.
First edition

ISBN 978-88-572-0588-5

Front cover
View of the Ghetto Nuovo

Facing title page
A Stroll in the Ghetto

On page 86
Campo del Ghetto Nuovo

Map of the Ghetto
Marco Zanella, Certosa di Pavia

© Photo Jody Sticca
© Pierreci Codess Coopcultura
with kind permission of Davide
Calimani, Francesco Turio Bhom,
Paola Baldari
© Photo Umberto Isman
© Photo Graziano Arici

Works owned by the
Soprintendenza are published
by permission of the Ministero
per i Beni e le Attività Culturali

The publisher is at the disposal
of the entitled parties as regards
all unidentified iconographic
and literary sources.

The publisher wishes to thank
Michela Zanon, Codess Cultura
and the Jewish Museum of Venice
for the images and the kind
collaboration.

Contents

7   The Ghetto of Venice

41   Itinerary

Appendix

88   Map

91   The Jewish Museum and its Library

92   Venetian Jewish Cuisine

94   Bibliography

95   Further Information

The Ghetto of Venice

● THE FIRST "GHETTO" IN THE WORLD

The Ghetto of Venice was the first of an infinite number throughout the world to be called by this name, which sadly became famous as a symbol of alienation, separation, segregation and discrimination. It was 29 March 1516: "The Jews must all live together in the Corte de Case that are in the Ghetto at San Girolamo; and so that they do not move around during the night [...] let two doors be built which are to be opened each morning at the Marangona" (the bell of San Marco whose toll announced the start of work at the Arsenale) "and to be closed each night at 12pm by four Christian guards [...] paid by the Jews at a fee deemed fair by our College". Some 700 Jews of German and Italian origin were confined to this unhealthy area in the *sestiere*, or quarter (the city is divided into six *sestieri*) of Cannaregio: near this area, people who had been executed were buried, and behind it was a muddy island.

There has been debate over the etymology of the word: that it derives from *Gitter*, in German meaning security bar; or from *Gasse*, laneway; or even from the Hebrew *get*, separation. However, it is simply the German guttural diction of the Venetian word *geto*, from the verb *gettare* (to cast): in the area there had been a copper foundry, abandoned around 1434: after too many fires – in 1100 at least five disastrous ones – the most dangerous activities were removed from the city centre (at the end of the thirteenth century, the glass furnaces were moved to Murano, and from 1460, all work involving gunpowder limited to the Arsenale). It was the *Casa del Geto*, which Dante called "Geto de rame del nostro Comun". Indeed, as there were two foundries (plus another 12 in the area, many of which were bronze foundries), the oldest part of the "serraglio of the Jews" was the

"Ghetto Nuovo", while the "Vecchio" was the more recent, an extension dating from 1541 to house the "Levantines". Then there was the "Nuovissimo", open (or closed?) in 1633: six *calli*, two doors, a bridge, four blocks, 32 houses; but they were more comfortable buildings, and there were even two palaces, the Treves and Vivante: it was almost a residential area.

However, overpopulation remained a serious problem: in the "peopled labyrinth of walls" (says the poet Percy Shelley), 50 metres at its narrowest and nowhere longer than 250, there were living areas with ceilings 1,75 metres high, created by halving rooms with a 4 metre ceiling. The area was surrounded by high walls, and doors and windows were walled; the guards were present day and night; there were two entries; the Jews even paid for two 24-hour patrol boats in the surrounding canals. This shameful situation lasted three centuries. On 7 July 1797, revocation of the segregation was an extreme act on the part of the *Serenissima*: Napoleon's soldiers were on the march; loss of freedom was imminent; seven months later, the *Horses* of San Marco went to Paris.

Pawn Shops
Numerous testimonies remain of the Jews' management of pawn shops. The *Esecutori contro la bestemmia* (Executors against Blasphemy) prosecuted those who sought loans over the established limit of three ducats, or at least those who resorted to threats to obtain them.

Every city of the Peninsula, with the exception of Livorno and Sabbioneta, had its ghetto; 39 years after the establishment of the ghetto in Venice, Pope Paul IV Carafa, in 1555, instituted the one in Rome: it was the last to be abolished, in 1870. Only with the unity of Italy, in 1866, did the Jews achieve the status of citizen. Then the Nazis in Central Europe reinstated their former segregated status, but for a far more sinister end: genocide.

Though it may seem peculiar, up to 130 years earlier, Venice was officially a "city without Jews". There is no substantiated proof to in-

TERMINATIONE
Et Ordini

DELL' ILLVSTR.^{MI} ET ECCELL.^{MI}
Signori Effecutori contra la Biaftemma,
Eletti dall'Eccelfo Confeglio di X.

1619. Adì 23. Marzo.

In materia delle eftorfioni, & violenze vfate
à Banchieri del Ghetto.

PAX | EVAN
TIBI | GELI
MAR | STA
CE | MEVS

Stampate per Antonio Pinelli,
Stampator Ducale.

A S. Maria Formofa, Jn Cale del Mondo Nouo.

dicate settlement in the past; even the name of the Island of the Giudecca derives from *zudegà*, "giudicato" (judged), and not "giudeo" (Jew) as might be thought: the name concerns a story about land granted as compensation to the family of a condemned man. It was prohibited, from 960, to take Jews on board ships of the Republic. They were accepted as workers (*strazzarioli*: sellers of used garments; doctors; money lenders, at controlled rates though) up to 1385, but they could not live in the city. They were forced to wear a visible sign of discrimination: an "O" sewn on their chest, a small wheel, as shown by Daniel Norsa in a painting in the church of Sant'Andrea in Mantua, one of the few works to portray a family of Jews.

In Venice however, the law regarding the "mark" was often evaded, so that in 1496 the small wheel became a yellow beret and from 1500 a red one, which was to be worn at all times, even in the summer, or the evader risked a month in prison and a fine of 50 gold ducats. The first authorisation to reside in the city dates from 1385; it was given to three money lenders from Nuremberg (and never did chance choose better names: Solomon, Jacob and Simon), who were permitted to practise in the city centre with several lenders (or *feneratores* as they were called) from Mestre, because after the Chioggia war (1379–81) the citizens of the *Serenissima* were in a bad state and Christians were not allowed to engage in money lending. In 1386, the Jews were even given a cemetery next to the Benedictine monastery of San Nicolò at the Lido: it measured 70 paces by 30.

Up to that time, the Church had avoided any contamination, and the merchant classes in power defended their monopoly on trade: trading rights were accorded only to those who had lived in the city for at least 25 years. However, in 1515, a year before inventing the Ghetto,

the *Serenissima* had conceded, to nine Jews, a used clothing stall each (new clothes were also sold, it was sufficient to mark them with a stain) at the Rialto markets for 5 thousand ducats. As we shall see, relations between *La Dominante* and the "Jews" had often been very vague.

● THE PALIMPSEST OF THE "SERRAGLIO OF THE JEWS"

Today the "serraglio", as vast as a handkerchief, is an unsurpassed palimpsest, a focal point of memories and a precious treasure: "Just 20 of the 450 people of the Venice Jewish community live here, where our institutions are", says Chief Rabbi Elia Enrico Richetti; however, the area has the highest concentration of extant Jewish cultural treasures. Almost five thousand souls (4,870 in 1654) were crammed there: two square metres per head, a density that was four times the average; 199 living units were registered in 1582, 368 in 1661. Originally on two levels, the houses around the Campo became taller: up to seven levels in the *calli*, but some went as high as nine; small skyscrapers ahead of their time. At the Correr Museum, Antonio Gaspari's design for the *Scala di [Moisé] Camis ebreo*, from the end of the seventeenth century, has 13 landings.

Every nation, ethnic groups having distinct rituals, built its own synagogue (called *Scole*); and if from the exterior many are anonymous, or almost invisible, each competed to make their own the richest and loveliest. Five synagogues rose between the sixteenth and seventeenth centuries: a rare historic and artistic compendium. They were often refurbished up to the nineteenth century, and today they form the heart of the Ghetto together with other ancient religious structures and the first Jewish museum in Italy (1955), which is also one of the most interesting because from the middle of the seventeenth century

The Ghetto seen from above

Documents record the presence of Jews from the first centuries of the Republic, also because Venice was a great centre of exchange between east and west. Jews, however, did not have the right to stay overnight in the city: only by virtue of a decree issued 130 years before the establishment of the Ghetto were they allowed to sojourn in the city. Later, all the Jews were confined to an unhealthy and uncomfortable quarter bordered by canals in the *sestiere* of Cannaregio.

to the beginning of the nineteenth century Venice had the monopoly on the production of ceremonial objects. The oldest synagogue is the German one, founded in 1528 in a building that possibly dates to the fifteenth century; three years later the Canton was established; then in 1538 the Levantine (rebuilt at the end of the seventeenth century), and in 1575 the Italian. The Spanish synagogue is from the first half of the seventeenth century, and like the Levantine, still officiating: one in the summer, the other in the winter. They have something in common with Venetian churches, apart from the absence of portraits of animate beings: although without definite proof, the Spanish synagogue is said to have been designed by Baldassarre Longhena (1598-1682), the architect of the Church of Santa Maria della Salute. There are also other smaller oratories (Mesullamìm, Kohanìm and Luzzatto), today annexed to the larger temples. No other city in the world has so many places devoted to the Jewish cult, as old and as close.

The rules
The first activity permitted for Jews was the management of pawn shops (there were perhaps three): Christians were still forbidden to lend money; other Jews dealt in commerce, especially with the east. Nevertheless, all activities were defined and regulated by the *condotte* (safe-conducts).

These buildings and the stories they hold still retain a great fascination. This is because, paradoxically, the Ghetto is a symbol of oppression and segregation, but also of values connected with freedom. The place attests to the fact that here the Jews were admitted, although in a contradictory way and for reasons of economic advantage, when a good part of Europe had for some time expelled them: England in 1290; France in 1306; in 1492 and 1497 Spain and Portugal, the Kingdom of Sicily and Sardinia. The Ghetto belonged to the Jews, even though they could not own buildings: in fact, in order to open it, the inhabitants were all moved in only three days, and at the same time rents were increased by a third. In the first seven years, 20 homes were carved out of 9, and annual rent

Regulaceo

E ORDENIS

Pellas quais se haverà
de Governar à

חברת עזרת אחים

Istituida no Anno 5472.
no K. K. de Talmud
Thorah.

IN VENEZIA , 1712.
Per Gioanni de'Paoli.
Con Licenza de' Super.

אהרן

משה

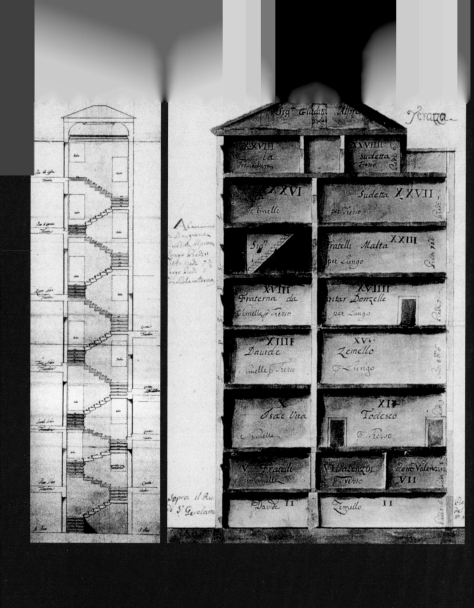

increased from 114 to 189 ducats, one third of which was tax free; Marco Michiel, the only nobleman who is known to have owned real estate in the area, rented his property for 15 ducats "before these Jews"; after their arrival the rent increased to 49 ducats (including the rental of the attic), and only 39.3 of the total was taxed.

• LIFE IN A MICROCOSM

When the Ghetto rose in Venice, Verona decreed there be a party; to the young puritanical rabbi Samuel Aboab it seemed the Jerusalem of the prophet Isaiah: he fought against the institution of a theatre, fearing "the holy city would transform into a whore". At the bridge on the *rio* and at the *sottoportego* on the Fondamenta di Cannaregio, the marks of the gate hinges can still be seen; at number 2912, on the architrave of a walled door, the words "banco rosso" (red bank) remain, although the date of the wording is unknown: the practice of money lending was identifiable by the colour of the receipts; in the Campo del Ghetto Nuovo there were also the "banco nigro" (black) and the "verde" (green), complementary to the credit centre which rose in 1619 in the Rialto; one *banco* was in the Calle del Forno, where sweets for *Pesach* were prepared at Easter. Not many *banchi* were visible, because the nobles feared being seen as they entered; they were built in stone, so that "light could not penetrate, dust could not infiltrate and thieves could not peer into". The *University of the Jews*, the internal institution in charge of collective life, had all that was needed for the almost self-managing suburb: a boat which collected refuse; water, supplied by the three wells in the Campo (it was the only square in Venice to have so

**Antonio Gaspari
(1670-1730)**

Project of a staircase for the Jew [Moisé] Camis
In the late seventeenth century, the Jewish community was expanding and buildings were becoming increasingly tall. The Ghetto stands out from other quarters in the city because of its tower-like houses.

many wells; they were rented to the Jews, but during the day the bearers shuttled externally also); lighting; and social structures. For Francesco Sansovino (1581), it was a "reduced municipality, almost a land of promise", in which Jews were "resting in very unique peace", "very well provided for and rich".

Life hummed there: there were intense exchanges with the city, and not only segregation. Alexandre-Toussaint Limojon de Saint-Didier, secretary to the ambassador to Louis XIV in Venice, noted (1680) that every nobleman could count Jews among his affectionate and trustworthy friends, and they were used for many reasons. Though with limitations, doctors could always leave, and others could obtain permission; among the most famous was David de Pomis, archiater to Doge Alvise Mocenigo, who was born in Spoleto in 1525, was at the court of the Orsini and the Sforza, graduated in Perugia and was traditionally a descendent of one of the four families brought to Rome by Titus; he made a speech before Pope Pius IV Medici, who appreciated it and allowed him to practise in Chiusi; but the Pope died five days later and Pope Pius V Ghislieri revoked the licence, so the doctor, scientist and literary man, formerly a rabbi, moved to the lagoon city.

At the time, a new public position arose for Daniel Rodriga: that of *Consul of the Venetian Nation* (meaning Jewish), also because he made Spalato (Split) Venice's first Adriatic port of call, avoiding the less hospitable Ragusa (Dubrovnik) and Ancona. Other notable figures lived at the same time: the poet Sara Copio Sullam, who had a lively literary coterie; the rabbi Leone da Modena, to whom even cardinals listened; Elia Levita, who in Rome taught Hebrew to Cardinal Egidio da Viterbo, and in Venice to Cardinal Domenico Grimani.

18

"A lovely comedy was produced" in 1531, and no "Christian could enter"; in 1632, Leone da Modena was Chapel master of the Academy of the Imperiti Bezokrenu et Zion, musicians who escaped Mantua; in 1726, in the house of Jacob della Viola, at *Purìm* (Carnival), a *pièce* was staged that mixed Hebrew, Italian and dialect; *L'estro poetico armonico* by Benedetto Marcello retains the echo of the 12 liturgical songs he had come to listen to and transcribe.

There was a theatre, a 25-room hotel, an inn and a hospital, distinctive shops for each nation, fruit, vegetable, candle and tobacco shops (in the mid-seventeenth century, there was only one other tobacco shop in Venice, at San Marco), wine shops, hat makers, butchers, barbers, menders, alchemists, book sellers: a city within a city. Another first for Venice was the Jewish press, which "invented income tax, statistics, State titles, book censorship, glass mirrors, and the lottery" (Morand), and even Internet's little "at" sign, the @ symbol: Venetian missives from the sixteenth century were found at Prato, in which the icon equals the capacity unit of an amphora.

Cohabitation with the *gentiles*, who were perhaps goaded by the sermons of the Franciscans, was not always easy: Friar Rufino urged them to "wring every bit of money from the Jews, and do not let them live". Nations divided the meagre spaces. The German Ashkenazi, given to money lending, the trade of used clothing and "making veils and bonnets", were flanked by the Levantines, who fluctuated more in terms of where they lived and were devoted to trade: indeed, they revived Venice's trade particularly in the Balkans and with the Turks. They wore turbans and flaunted opulence and splendour; the women were bejewelled, they wore "big pearls of great value" around their necks. Leone da Modena said: "They prayed Turkish style". Admit-

19

ted almost by a commercial treaty with the Republic, they had fewer restrictions than those crammed in the Ghetto Nuovo.

Bank tax, which at the beginning was 15 or 20 percent, fell to 5 percent in a century. Besides, there were many tributes: 10 thousand ducats each year for the Arsenale; 13 thousand for the *condotta* (safe-conduct) of 1537 (bank regulation); each renewal of a licence incurred a fee; the Jewish contribution was estimated to be 100 thousand ducats each year in 1625; 250 thousand in 1673, and they gave work to 4 thousand Christian artisans; between 1669 and 1700, 800 thousand ducats per year. They loaned for 13 months, from 3 ducats up, at a third of the estimated loan. Some of the most important loans did not always fare well; the government convinced the Jews to loan to Antonio Della Scala, Lord of Verona, who in the fourteenth century pawned his jewels: two years after his death in exile, they had still not been reimbursed. The (international) merchants fared better than the "bankers" (whose rate was imposed), forced to satisfy the poor, in a city which, contrary to many others, did not have Catholic pawnshops. The disparities created tensions. The Levantines were also monitored by the *Cinque Savi alla Mercanzia* (a board of trade), and the other groups by the *Ufficiali al Cattavèr*, who were half way between magistrates and policemen.

The residents

There are now only 20 Jews living in the Ghetto itself and the community consists of only 450 souls; however all the Jewish associations are located here. The main resource today is tourism, but there are also services and crafts.

The Levantines already found the Scola Tedesca, with its Palladian tympanum: the *aròn* is gilded, the ark where the sacred scrolls of the law are kept; many architectural elements remind one of the city's theatres from the same period; there are numerous didactic inscriptions. The pulpit is not positioned centrally, it was moved for static reasons; necessity deemed that the orientation was not correct and, be-

cause of pre-existing buildings, the room is trapezoidal; it is panelled in wood, and long benches line the walls as elsewhere in the city; the beautiful elliptical women's gallery above offsets the irregular shape of the room; the 10 Commandments are inlaid in mother-of-pearl. The only features recognisable from outside are the five large windows.

The adjacent Canton Synagogue is more refined, light and elegant: a gilded wooden frieze and eight relief medallions bear tempera paintings of biblical landscapes. It is a baroque and rococo masterpiece, with a particular feature: in the Medallion where Moses strikes water from the rock one sees an arm (Judaism forbids the portrayal of animate beings; however, in the two remaining catacombs in Rome there are many). We do not know if the name is derived from a family named Canton, or simply because it is in a corner, in Venetian *cantòn*; some differences in the rites suggest Provençal origins. Both synagogues are located on the top floor, so that those who attend them can see the sky and the stars.

Obviously the Levantines wanted a temple of their own, one that was impressive and majestic. They were rich: they built it in the centre of *their* Ghetto, Campiello delle Scuole, where the Scola Spagnola also stands, the Synagogue for the Nation from the west. Today's Levantine Synagogue does not date from the mid sixteenth century but from the late seventeenth; the name Longhena has been mentioned in reference both to this building and the nearby Spanish one: the façade recalls his style. It is non-Jewish in taste and almost completely devoid of inscriptions; the contribution of Andrea Brustolon, or the "Michelangelo of wood" (Balzac), is a possibility as he was active in Venice at the time; lamps and candlesticks compensate for the impos-

Andrea Mantegna
The Virgin of the Victory, 1495
tempera on canvas, 280 x 166 cm
Musée du Louvre, Paris
The painting was originally in Mantua. The Jewish banker Daniel Norsa paid for it as punishment for having removed a sacred image from the façade of his home, though with permission to do so.

sibility of having statues; rich woodwork decorates the ceiling and walls alternating with damask panels (recently replaced by less attractive fireproof fabric); polychrome marble; the twisted columns are perhaps a citation of Bernini in St. Peter's (Brustolon was in contact with him); above the *bimah*, the platform where scriptures and prayers are read, is a semi-hexagonal apse; below, in what was previously a reading room, the interiors of the *Midrash* Luzzatto have been housed since 1836. Next door is the Spanish Synagogue of the "Ponentine" Jews.

• THE THREE "NATIONS"

Alongside the original Ashkenazi from Eastern Europe and the Levantine Jews, who were the second group, the third Nation of the Ghetto was the "Ponentini", recognised as such in 1573, after their expulsions from the city in 1497 and 1550. They were destined to become the dominant group; they were the richest; many were *marrani* ("swine" in Castilian and in Portuguese): converts of Spanish origin, more or less openly returned to Judaism. They could "practice their rites" in the Ghetto; however, like the Levantines, they were free to "travel by sea, purchase, sell and and negotiate; transport back to Venice merchandise by sea or land, paying duties as other subjects", though they remained foreigners: tolerated and protected foreigners. Their synagogue, founded in 1584, is truly the most sumptuous: contrary to the temples in the Ghetto Nuovo and the Scola Levantina, marble is employed rather than common *marmorino*, a mixture of lime and crushed marble. Here again what we see today is the baroque seventeenth century version; on the ground floor a *midrash* was founded in 1733, a study room which today houses furnishings from the destroyed Scola Kohanim. In 1838 an organ was even installed and room

made for a choir: abolished 140 years later because foreign to Jewish rites; the *bimah* was returned to its original state. The Scola Spagnola, inconspicuous from outside, inside it is the largest and most scenographic. The *aròn* recalls the Cappella Vendramin, in the Castello district; and one of many epigraphs recalls how, during the siege of 1848, at the Jewish new year, an Austrian bomb hit the temple at prayer time, without however causing damage.

The last synagogue, though not in chronological order, is the Italian, a Nation that has never been recognised and has always been included with the German. In Campo del Ghetto Nuovo, the façade appears jutting out from the main body of the building, supported by four columns; the interior is panelled in wood; there are various inscriptions in gold or on black stone framed by stuccoes; the women's gallery was rebuilt in 1740; of all the synagogues it is perhaps the most austere and least refurbished.

Echoing in the surrounding *calli* are a thousand vicissitudes. Some of these bear the names of ancient Sephardic families: such as Barucchi, Corte Rodriga, or the extinct Mocato and Tubì. While the sixteenth century was restless, the seventeenth was glorious. In 1553, Pope Julius III, the pope who reinstated the Council of Trent after it was suspended by Pope Paul III in 1548, had copies of Jewish books and the Talmud burnt in Piazza San Marco; in 1563 it was decided that the Jews could stay only one more year in Venice for the payment of debts, but no longer with permission to lend money or to buy used clothing to sell; this decision was annulled; however, after the Battle of Lepanto (1571), the Banks were suspended for a year: the Senate decided that all Jews suspected of collusion with the Turks had to leave; the decision was revoked in 1573 and a new *condotta* was introduced

regulating their activities. Threats to withdraw licences from money lenders were made many times. However, in Venice economic requirements always influenced final decisions: Joseph Nasi, the heir of the wealthy Mendes family, which began from trade in Lisbon and Antwerp (spices, pepper and capital), was banished from the lagoon in 1533, but was readmitted in 1567, probably thanks to the sheer quantity of business he commanded in several countries and at least six capitals, first and foremost Constantinople. Then Maggino Gabrielli arrived (originally named Meir Zarfati), born in 1551, the son of a celebrated silk producer from Mantua, who invented strange beakers and transparent glass devices; he obtained patents from Pope Sixtus V, to whom he dedicated a poem in Hebrew, and together with Giovan Battista Guidoboni from Lucca devised an unusual method for doubling the silk harvest: drenched in malvasia, the eggs had to dry for two days in the breast of "a young woman". Namah Judah lived outside of the enclosure, exploiting patents for chemical compounds from which he also produced cinnabar; with another he produced white lead for the leading painters of the seventeenth century.

Ketubah (Marriage contract)
Several precious examples of these contracts are housed in the museum. They set down the rules for the marriage and eventual penalties should the wedding not take place. This one is between Mordechai Shalom Pissarro and Ester the daughter of Jehuda Chaim Sforni (1792).

Alongside the inventors came the false messiahs: one, the Ethiopian Dawid Reubeni, departed from here in 1524; he returned after six years travelling; a guest at Palazzo Contarini del Bovolo, of the famous spiral staircase, he came to a tragic end. In the mid seventeenth century one Shabbethaj Tsebhi from Smyrna was spreading illusions in the Ghetto, until he converted to Islam and became Mohamed Effendi.

Both are quite incredible figures: Reubeni, who travelled extensively in the Orient, claimed to be a descendent of an ancient tribe

and to have been sent to mobilise the ultimate forces against the Turks. Funds were raised for a trip to Rome where the Pope received him; he also travelled to Portugal and aroused the enthusiasm of the Marranos. Sanudo records his return to Venice in 1530; by now he was considered a suspicious individual and was interrogated. The verdict was "a fixation of the brain" and the conclusion was "tragic". In 1666, news reached Venice that one Zevi from Smyrna had risen as a Messiah; he preached an ascetic existence and made transformations in the liturgy; he had a certain following in Venice. The enthusiasm waned however, when Zevi accepted the title Effendi.

Levantine Synagogue
The synagogues or *Scole*, were built between the first quarter of the sixteenth and the middle of the seventeenth century by the various ethnic groups: the Ashkenazi (Jews following the rites from central and Eastern Europe), German, Canton, Italian, Levantine and Spanish synagogues.

● THE GOLDEN AGE OF PRINTING

It was the golden age of printing: Aldus Manutius had already used Hebrew characters; but in the sixteenth century David Bomberg, a Christian from Antwerp, published 200 works over a period of 30 years; his heir, Marco Antonio Giustiniani, published 90 in 7 years; and Giovanni Di Gara, who used Bomberg's characters, 100 in 40 years, up until 1609. In the mid sixteenth century 800 copies of a Talmud were published; the first Rabbinic Bibles appeared and the Babylonian Talmud in 12 volumes. Over time there were about a dozen publishers: all outside the Ghetto and rigorously Christian. Venice no longer offered only objects but also ideas; the city attracted intellectuals from all over the world: Galileo, Monteverdi, Luca Pacioli, Pietro Aretino, Erasmus of Rotterdam, to mention just a few.

Persecutions? Many, even though the inquisition in Venice was less severe than elsewhere. On the steps of the *aròn* of the Canton synagogue we can read: "1672, donated by Joshua Moshé, in suffrage for

his brother who was skinned like a kid goat". In 1636, two Jews stole 70 thousand ducats in Merceria: they were exposed by another Jew, the Ghetto was closed off and assaulted. Leone da Modena wrote a testimonial for the Jewess Dianora, accused of being a witch and sorceress: who knows how it ended?

In the Ghetto, 11 plaques (the oldest Jewish plaque however, is in the Jewish cemetery on the Lido and dates 1389; a cast can be seen in the museum): in front of the Canton synagogue, one recalls four executions at San Marco in 1480, for ritual homicide and contempt of religion. Another dating 1704, immediately entering from Cannaregio, forbids "any Jew or Jewess after becoming Christian to attend or practice under any pretext whatsoever in the Ghettos", and punishment is specified: "Prison, the galleys, ropes, the stocks"; the "serraglio of the Jews" was like a red light cinema: minors under the age of 16 were not allowed to enter the houses. On Friday evenings a non-Jewish trumpeter, paid by the Jews, sounded three times three calls at half hour intervals, signalling the start of *Shabbat*, and the cessation of all activity.

● THE HEYDAY OF THE GHETTO

The Ghetto had its heyday during the first half of the seventeenth century, though already a century before the Venetian rabbis had played an important role in the affair of the second marriage of Henry VIII of England, resulting in the Anglican schism: their recognised gui~~ing role, even beyond the lagoon, never waned.~~

~~…~~le~~…~~
spread; debt was on the ~~…~~zi, resorted to borrowing even outside of the walls to support the activities of their Banks. In 1631 the plague struck: 450 people died (they

are buried in a common grave on the Lido), and the first migrations towards Amsterdam or the Tyrrhenian occurred. For delivery from the scourge a new synagogue was built, the Mesullamìm: the *aròn* is housed today in the *Casa di Riposo* (Jewish home for the aged) in the Ghetto Nuovo, and one of the thirteen inscriptions on leather reads: "Come, let us rejoice and exult; in the streets of the city with drums and cymbals; enough Venice, enough of abandonment to mourning".

But the decline had begun. At the end of the seventeenth century the Levantine Jews pawned the silverware of the synagogue; the Jewish debt was at a million and 200 thousand ducats; it was bankruptcy. Venice was in alarm; the Senate and Great Council became involved; a plan was drawn up to settle the debts; it was accepted by the principal creditors (Francesco Labia, Marc'Antonio Venier and Nicolò Bembo), but the transaction was forced on another 60 creditors worth 300 thousand ducats. The senate passed a new *condotta*, 66 chapters, of which 33 were devoted to the refinancing and maintenance of the Banks, to which "all Jews were obliged": it turned out to be "the least favourable ever", and increased feelings of subjection.

There was little time left: in Venice as elsewhere, the Ghettos would fall. In the meantime the *Serenissima* had led the way in Italy: respecting the papal bull *Cum nimis absurdum* issued by Pope Paul IV in July 1555, ghettos had appeared everywhere. In Bologna it had lasted only a short while: all Jews were expelled in 1569, definitively in 1592; six gates in Ferrara, seven in Mantua, two (later three) in Florence, three in Modena, four in Padua (there was a Jewish guardian: it would happen in Venice too, in the two watch boxes still standing at Ponte sul Rio degli Ormesini). In Florence the houses reached 11 floors: a total of 598 rooms, 56 box-rooms and attics, 64 cellars, 46

shops. In Venice balconies and rooftop loggias were sometimes equipped with wooden roofs so as to provide extra space, and in 1582 there were *casoni*, almost like log cabins (nine of them, which was a record in the city), rented for between 5 and 16 ducats; in 1555, a report issued by the *Provveditori alla Sanità* (health authorities) complained of sub-letting to 10 or more persons in spaces which lacked fireplaces and services. In Verona the community paid for the room of each head of a family to have stairs, oven and toilet. The ethnic groups tended to remain separate; in Rome from 10 they became five, however, the Sicilian, Ashkenazi and Sephardic rites were celebrated separately. Jews had to choose between becoming converts, being expelled or joining the communities in the large cities, though in Emilia-Romagna 10 "serragli" were opened (or closed?), in Tuscany, one in Monte San Savino; and later than others, between 1724 to 1732, in Piemonte at Chieri, Carmagnola and Fossano.

Shoah Memorial

In Campo del Ghetto Novo, since 1979, a Monument has stood in memory of the Holocaust; it is called *the Last Train* and is by the Lithuanian artist Arbit Blatas, who lived in Venice for many years. There are seven bronze plaques and a symbol: the barbed wire of the concentration camps.

The gates were usually bolted at sunset and during the main Christian festivities; normally one could only travel with authorisation (in some Ghettos, if transfers exceeded three nights) and reporting to the authorities upon arrival; at times, when travelling, it was possible to avoid wearing distinctive emblems. Exchanges with the "other city" were always frequent; the range of activities – usually subordinate – was limited (and many communities became impoverished, especially the Roman Ghetto): only the rich and some intellectuals fared better.

The only faculty allowed was Medicine and those in Padua and Siena were highly attended. From 1702 it was forbidden to dance in the Roman Ghetto, except for wedding and circumcision celebrations;

in Mantua men and women could only dance together at weddings, however, they had to wear gloves; concerts and theatre performances were held during the evenings. The Ghetto period saw the birth of Hebrew sacred music.

The houses of the catechumen also date from this period, as well as compulsory sermons and many attempts at forced baptism; the first, in Roma (at Madonna dei Monti, today the Faculty of Architecture of Rome's Third University) dates from 1543.

Let us return to Venice. In 1777, Salomon Treves rented a building outside the enclosure, at San Geremia, for 500 ducats; and when the *Serenissima* fell, the act of surrender also bore the signatures of Mosé Luzzatto, Isaac Greco and Vita Vivante: certainly not Arian surnames, by now they had become part of the ruling class.

The cemetery on the Lido
From 1386, the Jews had a cemetery on the Lido, on land granted to them by the *Serenissima* at San Nicolò, close to a convent. It was used up until the Napoleonic reforms. The Jewish religion forbids interference with tombs or their removal.

After several petitions to the Austrian authorities, in 1798 Abramo Basevi opened the first of two Jewish owned jeweller's shops on the Rialto. Saul Levi Mortera carried out the first census of the "serraglio": 1626 souls; 421 heads of family: 38 out of 100 born outside of Venice, 85 sellers of rags; 11 Germans, almost all beggars or servants; 16 employed in three Banks, 47 engaged in religion and education; the most important names among the merchants, textile manufacturers and ship owners: Treves, Vivante, Curiel, Errera, Gentili, Bonfil, Todesco and Malta. The structures were in very poor conditions after "the gates had been unhinged, smashed with axes and burned amid music and dancing of Jews with Christians", restoration was urgently needed.

Then the Austrians arrived and with them some of the restrictions returned, until 1866.

The wells

There is an abundance of water in the Ghetto; in the Ghetto Nuovo alone there are three ancient well-curbs, the property of the Brolo family: their coat-of-arms can still be seen on them. The Jews had to pay this family for the precious resource. The well-curb phographed on the right is in the centre of Campo del Ghetto Nuovo, the hub of the area, where there are three synagogues and the museum, the first of its kind in Italy.

• THE GHETTO TODAY

Today the Ghetto has become a popular attraction for both citizens and tourists. Since 1990 visits to the museum, directed by Michela Zanon, and the synagogues (three are normally open) are organised by Coperativa Codess, now called Coopcultura: the organisation invests part of the proceeds in restorations so as to improve service to the public; these are added to funds from the community and public bodies aimed at the rehabilitation of the Ghetto's spaces; thus, each year new discoveries are made: ancient wardrobes, floors, even walls with fragments of frescos.

In the words of Michela Zanon: "The real boom of visitors came in 2001: 90 thousand, alongside 4 thousand free entrances; after September 11th we have not seen any more Americans. In 2009, we tore off 68 thousand tickets: half have been foreign tourists, and more than 15 thousand school children". The bookshop of the museum is the best stocked among among the Jewish bookshops of Venice, and perhaps not only: over three thousand titles.

The museum is undergoing an extensive refurbishment at present: soon the precious collection fabrics will also be on show with over one thousand exhibits. "The oldest piece is by Stella Perugia, who died in 1673, a *parochet* which is placed in front of the Holy Ark, a golden yellow embroidery on a blue background", explains Michela Zanon. There are also some precious ancient *kettubbot*, marriage contracts dating from the first century written in Aramaic. There is even a ghost story, the spirit of a seventeenth century rabbi called Avraham who has been seen by many floating above the Ghetto: a cleaner is said to have won 100 thousand lire at that time playing lotto, then she quit her job for fear.

For some time now a group of Orthodox Jews has settled in the ghetto: members of the Lubavich sect. They have a school in the Campo, and they run a restaurant called Gam Gam. It has competition however: the Jewish home for the aged now has less residents than before, one of the floors has been turned into a guest house, with 28 beds in 14 rooms; and on the ground floor the restaurant seats 100, it also has a garden; it is opposite the older Locanda del Ghetto, with five rooms, next to the Italian Synagogue (indeed the synagogue is its roof).

In Campo del Ghetto Nuovo, the true life and heart of the Ghetto where many events are organised, also by the Jewish community, we find the last plaques that have been installed: they recall the *Shoah*, 7 bronze panels by the Lithuanian artist Arbit Blatas, who spent many years in Venice; he also created the Monument to the 256 Venetians who died in the concentration camps, *L'ultimo treno* ("The Last Train"), from 1979: name, surname and age of the victims.

In the museum's new layout the place of honour is reserved to a photo: amid a jubilant crowd in the Ghetto, a Jew, a colonel in the Jewish Brigade that joined the British forces, carries the scrolls of the Torah back to the Spanish Synagogue in 1945; next to it, an original *sukkà* from 1820, under which the Feast of Tabernacles was celebrated. All around are many artisans and artists' studios.

In 1850, Théophile Gautier (1811-1872) described the Ghetto: "A Venice that is in no way like the coquettish city found in watercolours". In many ways it is still so.

Itinerary

Ghetto Nuovo

Campo del Ghetto Nuovo is the heart of the area. For centuries it was forbidden for Jews to live in the city centre; the first permits, connected with commercial activities, date from 1385. The decree that established the Ghetto dates from 29 March 1516: in an unhealthy part of the city where there were foundries (hence the name: *Geto* – from the verb *gettare*, to cast –, in the German diction); it was the first ghetto in the world to be called by this name. It is divided into three parts: the first is the Ghetto Nuovo, older than the second, the Ghetto Vecchio; the third is the Ghetto Nuovissimo, opened in 1633.

Campo del Ghetto Nuovo

Isolation, and therefore shame, lasted for three centuries: segregation was abolished shortly before the arrival of Napoleon in 1797; this event is recalled in a memorial in the centre of Campo del Ghetto Nuovo. But it was only with the founding of the Kingdom of Italy that Jews achieved real equality with the rest of Italian citizens. Today not more than 20 Jews live in the Ghetto, but all the Community's institutions are located here; there are shops, restaurants, bars and even two small hotels, as well as the five synagogues, the museum, the library and the Jewish home for the aged. The well-curbs in the square still bear the coat-of-arms of the Brolo family, that owned them at the time the area became the "serraglio of the Jews".

Gradually, life developed in the Ghetto. In 1582, 199 living units were registered here; by 1661 they had become 368. Jews of different origin could organise themselves into "Universities", small autonomous entities, each one with its own rabbi and synagogue. Between the sixteenth and seventeenth century five synagogues rose in the Ghetto. Jews were forbidden to own land and real estate, and could not exercise certain professions or hold public office; the practice of medicine, small commercial activities and crafts were tolerated. Therefore schools, workshops and pawn shops were established, alongside trade activities of every type.

Sotoportego and pawn shops

The *sotoportego* (literally "under arcade") is one of the most typical features of the Venetian urban structure. It is a passage that connects *calli* or streets directly through the main body of a building, usually cutting a passage the height of the ground floor. Very often a *sotoportego* is the only access to a courtyard or small square. Under the portico photographed above we find the "banco rosso", one of the three original pawn shops that were established in the Ghetto. There were others in the city. Since Christians were forbidden to earn interest from loans, Venice assigned to the inhabitants of the Ghetto the role of lending sums of money in lieu of pawned goods, thus the pawn shops (red, green or black according to the colour of the receipt), which transformed this area into an important place of exchange between Christians and Jews.

Scola Italiana

The synagogues are located on the upper floors of buildings and it is not easy to identify them from the outside; some characteristic elements, however, are recognizable, such as the typical five windows in a row. Of the five existing synagogues in the Ghetto, rites of worship are still practised in the Scola Spagnola, used as a summer synagogue, and the Scola Italiana (in this photo), used as a winter synagogue. It is a local peculiarity that the word *Scola* – originally used for the places of worship of the city's Christian confraternities – is preferred to the word synagogue. Another particular characteristic of the Venetian synagogues is the rectangular layout, with the Holy Ark facing the *bimah* on the shorter sides while benches line the longer sides. The walls are lined with biblical quotations written in Hebrew, lamps in brass and silver, a great quantity of precious fabrics and red awnings.

Holocaust Monument

The Monument, by Arbit Blatas, was set on the wall to the left side of Campo del Ghetto Nuovo on 25 April 1980. There are seven bronze plaques and a symbolic barbed wire. It reminds passers-by and visitors of the tragedy of deportation and the concentration camps. Next to the monument is the Jewish home for the aged, built in 1890 and still in operation today. It was from here that the mournful cortège of deportees departed during the Nazi-fascist persecution.

The Last Train

Again by Arbit Blatas,
a Lithuanian who spent
many years in Venice, this
work dates from 1979
and recalls the *Shoah*.
256 people were deported
from the Ghetto; their
names are listed on this
monument, which is also in
Campo del Ghetto Nuovo.
The Last Train recalls
what was the final journey
for many of them.
Very few returned from
the concentration camps
at the end of the
Second World War.

Building in the Ghetto

Overcrowding soon became a huge problem: in this "peopled labyrinth of walls" (as the poet Shelley describes it) one can still find apartments with ceilings only 1,75 metres high, obtained by halving rooms four metres high. It is a curious fact that Venice passed from being a city without Jews (from 960 onward, they were even forbidden to embark on the Republic's ships) to hosting a large community crammed into a limited space; density reached its height in 1654, when 4,870 people were recorded living in the Ghetto: there were only two square metres per person, a density four times the average of the rest of the city.

2879

Ghetto Vecchio

Crossing the bridge on Rio degli Agudi one enters the Ghetto Vecchio, an area granted to the Levantine Jews in 1541; despite centuries of isolation it has maintained typical Venetian characteristics; indeed it comprises a long central *calle* once called the "strada maestra" (main street), where the workshops were located, and the essential services for community life. This long street, intersected perpendicularly by smaller alleys, leads to a small square, the Campiello delle Scuole.

Plaque in the Ghetto Vecchio

At the beginning of Calle del Ghetto Vecchio, on a building on the left hand side, a stone plaque carries a decree issued in 1704 by the *Esecutori contro la* *Bestemmia* (Executors against Blasphemy). It prohibits converted Jews from entering the Ghetto, and specifies the penalty for disobedience as well as the reward for those who reported transgressors.

Buildings in the Ghetto

Aiming to accommodate the greatest number of people in the limited space available, houses in the Ghetto developed upwards, giving rise to high buildings, of up to eight floors, with ceilings lower than average. The Ghetto is indeed made up of tower-like houses, with irregular and discontinuous profiles. One can notice how the façades are often pierced by small windows at odd levels; the ground floors were used for workshops and pawn shops.

The Parish of Sant'Alvise

The city of Venice is divided into *sestieri* and the *sestieri* into parishes; the Ghetto is part of the parish of Sant'Alvise, in the *sestiere* of Cannaregio, at least according to today's layout. The three sections of the Ghetto are separated by as many bridges. There are 416 bridges in Venice: 308 in stone, 59 in cast iron, 19 in wood; of these, 337 are public bridges.

The Gates of the Ghetto

Robust gates closed off
the entrances to the Ghetto
and every evening
the inhabitants had to
return and remain enclosed
there until the following
morning. The guards were
paid by the community;
during the day, however,
exchanges occurred
with the rest of the city
and commerce and
activities were intense
within the enclosure.
With the passing of time
the number of inhabitants
continued to grow,
from 700 they became
4870 by 1654.
Therefore, two additions
were made to the Ghetto
originally established
in 1516, one in 1541 and
the other in 1633; both
areas were also enclosed
by gates.

Ponte del Ghetto Nuovo

The Ghetto Nuovo
occupies one of the 118
islands of Venice
completely: there are three
bridges, two in cast iron
and one in wood.

Ponte del Ghetto Nuovissimo

Established in 1633 for the rich Ponentine merchant families who arrived at that time, the Ghetto Nuovissimo was the latest addition to the Ghetto. The area is smaller than the other parts of the Ghetto and is located where two canals – Rio di San Girolamo and Rio del Ghetto Nuovo – meet. The area is made of two perpendicularly intersecting alleys linking three blocks; it consisted only of houses, there were no workshops or synagogues.

Jewish home for the aged and Ponte del Ghetto Vecchio

The Ghetto contains all the Jewish institutions of the city, including the home for the aged, founded in 1890.
Today there are very few inmates; one of the unoccupied floors has been converted into a small hotel, with 14 rooms. On the ground floor there is also a restaurant with a pleasant garden.
The home for the aged is in a corner of Campo del Ghetto Nuovo, which is the very heart of the quarter.

Daniel Norsa

In this fragment of a painting, the banker Daniel Norsa from Mantua wears the distinctive sign that Jews were obliged to wear: a "wheel" on their clothes. In Venice this rule was widely disobeyed and the wheel was later substituted with a cap, first yellow and later red, to be worn regardless of the season. Norsa was made to pay Mantegna for a religious painting because he had cancelled a sacred image from the façade of his house, though he had acquired all the necessary permits.

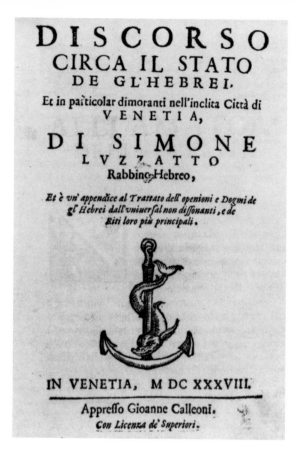

DISCORSO
CIRCA IL STATO
DE GL'HEBREI.

Et in particolar dimoranti nell'inclita Città di
VENETIA,

DI SIMONE
LVZZATTO
Rabbino Hebreo,

Et è un' appendice al Trattato dell' openioni e Dogmi de gl' Hebrei dall' universal non dissonanti, e de Riti loro più principali.

IN VENETIA, M DC XXXVIII.

Appresso Gioanne Calleoni.
Con Licenza de' Superiori.

Simone Luzzatto

Discorso circa il Stato de gl'Hebrei et in particolar dimoranti nell'inclita Città di Venetia ("Discourse on the conditions of the Jews, and in particular those living in the proud city of Venice"),1638.

Though printing was an exclusively Christian activity, by the sixteenth century the publication of Jewish material was a flourishing activity in Venice outside of the Ghetto. This discourse is by Simone Luzzatto, an important Venetian rabbi.

When numerous Jews were being expelled from other Italian and European cities, he wrote this pamphlet addressed to the Doge with the aim of convincing him to decide against an edict of expulsion of the Venetian Jews.

63

Giulio Morosini

The Jew Samuel Nahmias (1612–1687), later baptised, is portrayed in this old engraving. As all converts he changed his name and was called Giulio Morosini. He took holy orders as a Capuchin friar and in a book published in 1683 he described his spiritual journey and spoke of life in the Ghetto.

Simone Calimani

In Venice there was an important production of educational and religious texts; Simone Calimani, grammarian, poet, playwright, translator, and a rabbi in Venice, where he was born, in 1782 wrote *Esame o sia catechismo ad un giovane israelita*, a text in dialogue form between a teacher and his pupil.

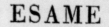

ESAME

O SIA

CATECHISMO

AD UN GIOVANE ISRAELITA

ISTRUITO NELLA SUA RELIGIONE

COMPOSTO

DA SIMONE CALIMANI

RABINO IN VENEZIA.

EDIZIONE TERZA

CORRETTA CON AGGIUNTE

זכר עשה לנפלאותיו
יעיר איון לשמוע בלמודים
בכל סקומות ממשלתו יחי
אדיננו המלך לעולם
טריאסטי החקמ"נ

IN VERONA

DALLA SOCIETA' TIPOGRAFICA EDITRICE

1821.

שמע 'ש'ר'א'ל' ה' אלדינו ה' אחד

Lorenzo da Ponte

A portrait by Nathaniel Rogers dated 1820, housed in Museo del Cenedese in Vittorio Veneto. Lorenzo da Ponte (his original name was Emanuele Conegliano, he was born in Ceneda, today known as Vittorio Veneto, in 1749, and died in 1838 in New York), was the librettists of the "Italian operas" by Mozart: *Le nozze di Figaro*, *Don Giovanni* and *Così fan tutte*. Though born a Jew, he converted and even took holy orders though he lived a licentious and adventurous life. In the United Sates he held the first university chair of Italian.

Edict of the Cattaveri

Dated 30 January 1732. There were numerous branches of judiciary in Venice; at first the Ghetto was controlled by the *Cattaveri*, an insitution half way between a police force and magistrates, and later also by the *Cinque Savi alla Mercanzia* (a board of trade).

IL SERENISSIMO PRENCIPE
FA' SAPERE,
Et è d'Ordine degl' Illustrissimi, & Eccellentissimi Signori
CATTAVERI.

 HE restando per più Leggi a loro Eccellenze comesa la sovraintendenza nelli Sanseri del Ghetto, commandata perciò con Decreto 1563. Primo Zugno à loro Precessori l'elettione di dodeci Sanseri Ordinarij nel Ghetto stesso, quali Carichi benche in forza di posteriori ordinazioni venduti al Publico Incanto, & esercitati in parte da Proprietarij, & in parte da Sostituti con il peso delle Decime annesse, e dovute, mai però possano da veruno essercitarsi senza un Mandato di Sue Eccellenze, & esendo a questi tempi invalso gravissimo abuso, che molti Ebrei si fanno lecito di far li Sanseri in pregiudizio delli dodeci, che con titolo legittimo s'esercitano, e soccombono a suoi aggravij, e che oltre a questo alli stessi dodeci Sanseri non vengono corrisposte quelle Utilità, che dalle Leggi, e da Publiche Tariffe sono permessi; il che causa la desolazione delli dodeci Sanseri stessi; & è contro la Publica intenzione. Perciò

Fanno Sue Eccellenze publicamente sapere, & intendere, che non vi sia Persona alcuna così Ebreo, come d'altra condizione che ardisca di far il Sensale nel Ghetto, e molto meno, che da chi incombe, non siano corrisposte l'Utilità tutte legittime, e particolarmente espresse nell'ultima Tariffa a stampa esistente nel loro Eccellentissimo Magistrato gia formata dagl' Illustrissimi, & Eccellentissimi Signori Inquisitori sopra le Tariffe alli dodeci Ebrei Sanseri Ordinarij nel Ghetto, come è di tutta Giustizia, e ciò sotto quelle pene, che a Sue Eccellenze pareranno in conformità delle trasgressioni che si rilevassero.

Il presente per la sua essecuzione sia stampato, e publicato, e resti pur affisso ne luochi più colpicui nel Ghetto ad universale notizia; Ne sia anco consignata Copia alli Capi di Strazzaria accid non se ne finga in tempo alcuno ignoranza per la sua essecuzione.

Dat. dal Magistrato Eccellentissimo di Cattaver li 26. Gennaro 1731.

(*Lunardo Querini Cattaver.*

(*Iseppo Minio Cattaver.*

Gio: Maria Marinoni Nod.

Adi 30. Gennaro 1731. M. V. Publicato nelli Ghetti di questa Città.

Stampato per Z. Antonio. & Almorò Pinelli Stampatori Ducali.

German Synagogue

The German Synagogue
is located in Campo
di Ghetto Nuovo,
diagonally opposite the
home for the aged. It was
begun in 1529 and is
identifiable from outside
by the five windows that
look onto the Campo.
It is trapezoidal in form
and along the longer sides
the *aròn* and *bimah* face
each other: the latter,
unlike those in the other
four synagogues in the
Ghetto, is on the same
level as the congregation.
The irregular floor-plan of
the Scola Grande Tedesca
is rendered harmonious by
the later inclusion of an
elliptical women's gallery,
the decoration of the walls
in marmorino plaster work
and the Decalogue written
in golden letters on a red
background which runs
around the perimeter of
the hall.

Canton Synagogue

It was the second synagogue to be built, in 1531, and is considered to be the most refined. It is also the most mysterious: it is not known whether it was built privately for the Canton family or was called so simply because it is on a corner (*cantòn* in Venetian). This light and elegant synagogue has a gilded frieze and eight medallions in relief with tempera paintings of biblical landscapes. In one of these paintings an arm of Moses is visible: this is quite unique since the Hebrew religion forbids the portrayal of animate beings.

Levantine Synagogue

Founded in 1541, it was rebuilt during the second half of the seventeenth century. Though there are no documents that clearly testify to the fact, it is presumed that Baldassarre Longhena was involved in the project: stylistic features of his appear in the façade. The impressive pulpit is attributed to Andrea Brustolon.

The two lamps are interesting, as are the *aròn*, in polychrome marble, both rich and austere at the same time, and especially the pulpit, which is of great effect, sumptuous and oriental in a typical seventeenth century manner.

The external façade is marked by a series of windows. Inside, the entrance has a rectangular shape: on the right side there is the *Midrash* Luzzatto, a small room to study and pray; to the left is the staircase leading to the hall of worship and the women's gallery.

Italian Synagogue

Built in 1575, it is the simplest of the Venetian synagogues; it is also the most luminous, thanks to the five broad windows that open onto the southern end of the Campo.
It is the most austere because it lacks the gold leaf ornamentation of the two Ashkenazi synagogues. The Scola Italiana is also dominated by the *aròn* and the *bimah*, which is in a particularly high position with respect to the congregation, and lend a harmonic sobriety to the entire rectangular layout.

Spanish Synagogue

This is the largest of the Venetian synagogues and can be dated to the second half of the sixteenth century. It underwent several restorations: one was in 1635, possibly on a plan by Baldassarre Longhena, and another was carried out towards the end of the nineteenth century. Coming from Campo del Ghetto Nuovo, one can notice its large finely carved wooden door and above them the big windows with coloured glass. The hall is rectangular with an elliptical women's gallery similar to the one in the German synagogue. The benches for the congregation are positioned along the longer walls, the *aròn* and *bimah* are on the short sides. The floor is paved in white and grey marble and the ceiling is finely decorated.

The synagogues in the Ghetto, as one can see in this image of the Spanish Synagogue, are bifocal because of lack of space, the *aròn* (the ark that holds the Scrolls of the Law) and the *bimah* (the pulpit used for prayer) are opposite each other. This is a repetition of Venetian models of the time. Also for this reason the complex can be considered a unique specimen and a precious treasure of Jewish culture.

Jewish Museum

The Venice Ghetto has the first Jewish museum in Italy, opened in 1955. It contains numerous treasures of art and culture, ritual silverware and an important collection of fabrics, dating back to the seventeenth century, and *ketubahs*, old marriage contracts. Since 1990 it is managed by a cooperative. The museum also houses the Jewish book shop – perhaps the best stocked store of its kind in Italy, with over three thousand titles – and a restaurant.

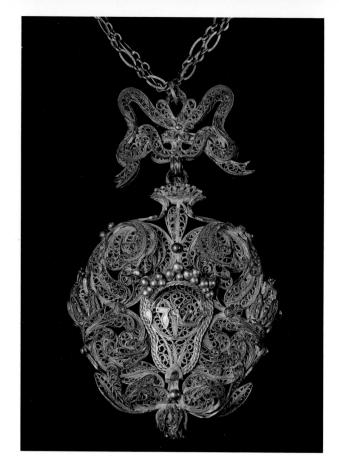

Silverware

The museum contains authentic masterpieces such as these: on the left, from the workshop of Angelo Scartabello in Este, an *atarah* and *rimmonim* from the eighteenth century, silver and gold: that is, a crown that confers royal dignity to the Torah, the scrolls of the Law, and the ornaments placed on the upper part of the supports onto which they are rolled.

The other object, nineteenth century from Piedmont, is a *shaddai*, in silver filigree and gilded silver: it is a precious amulet which was placed in the cradle of newly born children.

**Plate for the Seder
of Pesach**

Second half of the
nineteenth century,
France (?)
In silver and hard stones,
the *Seder* plate is central
to the meal for the
ceremony of *Pesach*,
which commemorates
the liberation of the people
of Israel from the captivity
in Egypt.

Cemetery on the Lido

In 1386, the Jews obtained land on the Lido for their cemetery: next to the Benedictine monastery of San Nicolò, 70 paces by 30. After being abandoned in 1938, with the racial laws, it was only in 1999 that a complex restoration of the cemetery began. Over one thousand tombstones have been catalogued, dating from 1550 to the beginning of the eighteenth century. The cemetery currently in use is accessible from via Cipro 70, but the old cemetery can be visited at given times. In Hebrew the cemetery is known as *Bet a Chaìm*, the House of the Living. The Jewish religion forbids the exhumation of the dead.

Appendix

Map

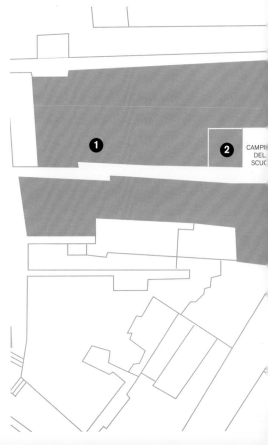

1. Stone plaque in the Ghetto Vecchio
2. Scola Spagnola
3. Scola Levantina
4. Scola Luzzatto
5. Scola Leon da Modena
6. Midhrash Vivante
7. Scola Italiana
8. Scola Canton
9. Scola Tedesca
and Jewish Museum
10. Stone plaque in the Ghetto Nuovo
11. Home for the aged
12. Holocaust memorial
13. Scola Mesullamìn
14. Scola Luzzatto
(original site)
The Last Train Monument
15. Scola Kohanìm
Coffee shop and bookshop

CAMPI
DEL
SCUO

GHETTO

Tronchetto   Stazione   Guglie
                           S. Marcuola
Piazzale Roma   Rialto

S. Marco

S. Giorgio

Giudecca

6

GHETTO VECCHIO

3   **5**

13   **12**

11

7   GHETTO NUOVO

10

14

8

16

9   **15**

The Jewish Museum and its Library

Jewish Museum

In the Campo del Ghetto Nuovo, the Jewish Museum of Venice is housed in one of the oldest Venetian synagogues: it is a small but splendid museum founded in 1955 by the Venetian Jewish community.
It contains precious objects, significant examples of the goldsmith's art and textiles dating to between the sixteenth and nineteenth century.
The collection includes objects connected with the Jewish cult and festivals, from the *Shabbat*, the day dedicated to prayer, to *Pesach*, the Jewish Easter. There are curious relics, such as wedding contracts (*ketubahs*) in the form of parchment handwritten and coloured in tempera, with rules for the safeguarding of women in case of dissolution of marriage, as per the Jewish tradition. The museum is also the reference point for visiting the synagogues and the Jewish cemetery at the Lido.

Library

Founded in 1974, the Library was officially established in 1981. It contains the books and archival holdings of the Venetian Jewish community and aims to contribute to the spread of knowledge on Jewish culture and civilisation and in particular the history of the Jews in Venice and in Italy.

Venetian Jewish cuisine

Jewish cuisine hinges on the concept of *kosher* food, meaning "appropriate" according to the dictates of the Torah applied to everyday life by a rabbi. Without going into detail, the following are prohibited: pork, as is commonly known, but also rabbit, eel, shellfish, and meat in general cooked in milk and in its derivatives, cream and butter. This is the case everywhere, but Venice is peculiar because in no other place in the world there has been such an overlapping of customs.

In the Ghetto the plain cuisine of the Ashkenazi Jews, who came from Germany, mixed with the exuberant cuisine of the Sephardic Jews, who were from southern France and Spain, not to mention the contribution of the Levantines and the many other heterogeneous influences connected with maritime trade. The emblematic dish of Venetian Jewish cuisine is *sarde in saor*,

a sweet and sour recipe in which anchovies are marinated with vinegar and onion mixed with raisins and pine nuts – but there are many other specialities from this very particular ethnic tradition. Food traditions and *kosher* assume even greater importance during Jewish festivals. For example, during *Hanukkah* (or *Chanukkah*), Jewish families all over the world, after having lit the ritual candelabra, eat a great variety of different food according to their culture of reference; famous dishes of the Israelite

tradition include *sufganiyot* and *latkes*, potato pancakes.

The Jewish religious calendar includes typical and complex rituals such as those of Easter (*Pesach*), also called "Feast of unleavened bread", which recalls the flight from Egyptian slavery. At the table, the peak is the evening prior to the first day, when the ritual meal, which has remained practically identical throughout the centuries, is consumed. During the first two evenings, as well, there is a precise order to eating food and to prayer during dinner, which is called *Seder*, a Hebrew word

meaning "order", and there is a narration of the entire story of the conflict with the pharaoh, the 10 plagues and the final flight following the story of *Haggadah* of *Pesach*.

Where to eat kosher
Panificio Volpe

Calle del Ghetto Vecchio
Cannaregio, 1143
Tel. (+39) 041 715178
This bakery sells Jewish sweets typical of the Venice Ghetto such as: "orecchiette di Amman", filled with fruit; "bisce" with the characteristic "S" shape; "zuccherini" and "azzime dolci" in a doughnut shape. It also sells cookies of matzoh meal, macaroons and almond cakes. All sweets are made with ingredients sanctioned by *kosher* rules.

Cafeteria of the Venice Jewish Museum
Campo del Ghetto Nuovo, 2902
Tel. (+39) 3401046858
Make a stop here for a variety of *kosher* refreshments.

Gam-Gam Jewish Restaurant
Sotoportego del Ghetto
Tel. (+39) 041 715284
The menu adheres strictly to the food guidelines the Bible handed down to the Israelites.

Le Balthazar
Campo del Ghetto Nuovo
Cannaregio, 2873c
Tel. (+39) 3460391183
In the heart of the Jewish Ghetto, the restaurant offers typical Jewish cuisine, either from a fixed price or *à la carte* menu. Visitors experiencing a *Shabbat* here, Friday evening or *Shabbat* lunch, will enjoy a welcoming atmosphere with products under close rabbinical scrutiny by the head rabbi of the Jewish community in Venice.

Bibliography

R. Calimani, *The Ghetto of Venice*, New York 1987

L. Modena, M.R. Cohen, *The autobiography of a seventeenth-century Venetian rabbi: Leon Modena's Life of Judah*, Princeton 1988

H.AE. Adelman, *Success and failure in the seventeenth century Ghetto of Venice: the life and thought of Leon Modena, 1571-1648*, Ann Arbor 1990

V.B. Mann (edited by), *Gardens and ghettos: the art of Jewish life in Italy*, Berkeley, Los Angeles, Oxford 1990

U. Fortis, *Jews and synagogues, Venice, Florence, Rome, Leghorn: a practical guide*, Venezia 1991

D.B. Ruderman (edited by), *Essential papers on Jewish culture in Renaissance and Baroque Italy*, New York 1992

D.B. Ruderman (edited by), *Preachers of the Italian Ghetto*, Berkeley, Los Angeles, Oxford 1992

B. Arbel, *Trading nations: Jews and Venetians in the early-modern eastern Mediterranean*, Leiden, New York, Köln 1995

B. Pullan, *The Jews of Europe and the Inquisition of Venice, 1550-1670*, London 1997

R. Calimani, G. Sullam Reinisch, C. Vivante, *Venice: guide to the synagogues, museum and cemetery*, Venice 2001

R.C. Davies, B. Ravid (edited by), *The Jews of Early Modern Venice*, Baltimore 2001

A. Sacerdoti, *The guide to Jewish Italy*, Venice 2003

A.-V. Sullam Calimani, R. Calimani, *The Venetian Ghetto*, Milan 2005

D.N. Myers, *Acculturation and its discontents: the Italian Jewish experience between exclusion and inclusion*, Toronto 2008

M. Brenner, *A short history of the Jews*, Princeton 2010

Further Information

Jewish Museum
Address: Campo del Ghetto Nuovo
Cannaregio, 2902/b
Tel. (+39) 041 715359
museoebraico@codesscultura.it
www.museoebraico.it

Opening Hours
June-September: Monday-Friday, Sunday
10.00-19.00.
October-May: Monday-Friday, Sunday
10.00-17.30.
Closed on Saturday and Jewish festivals.